LinkedInsider Marketing

How to Use LinkedIn as
Social Media Capital in Your Business

By R. Scott Hall

Table of Contents

Introduction.. 1

Benefits of Using LinkedIn 3

Misconceptions about LinkedIn............................. 7

Getting LinkedIn 11

Quick Tips for Success... 17

LinkedIn Checklist... 19

Questions You Should Ask....................................... 21

Conclusion.. 23

Next Steps... 25

Recommended Resources.. 27

About Scott

Scott is an expert in online marketing and implementation across emerging social media platforms. His 20 years of experience at digital pioneering companies like CompuServe (AOL), Macmillan Digital Publishing (Pearson) and Nokia Corporation (Microsoft) lends breadth and depth of practical experience in technology and media. He consults, strategizes and teaches entrepreneurs, coaches, consultants and SMBs to build social media capital. His first book, "The Blog Ahead" - was published as an overview and analysis of the growing social media landscape and its impact on business and the media.

Introduction

When it comes to using social networks to market their company, many business owners have already heard about the two biggest: Facebook and Twitter. Many are already using those networks to market their brand and promote their business, yet many of these same business owners don't have a LinkedIn profile yet. Why? It's certainly not because LinkedIn is new to the scene. In fact, out of the three, LinkedIn is the oldest of the social networking sites. Twitter was established in 2006, Facebook was launched in 2004 and LinkedIn was launched in 2003.

It's also not because LinkedIn lacks any of the benefits the other two major social networking sites offer. LinkedIn actually holds more benefits over both for the small business owner. It's much more in-depth than sending out Tweets and it doesn't include distracting games like Facebook does. The biggest reason why business owners don't use LinkedIn is simply because they are unaware of the benefits, as well as how to use it. Add to that the myths surrounding LinkedIn and it's quite easy to see why LinkedIn is the least popular of the three.

This guide will burst through the myths and actually show you how to use it and what to do to make the most of it. For those that don't know we'll also take a look at the many benefits that come with using LinkedIn.

Benefits of Using LinkedIn

The main benefit of using LinkedIn is that it's going to translate into more profits for your company. The website can also offer your business more than an increase in its bottom line.

Here is a short rundown of some of the benefits of using LinkedIn:

Grow your network and target your network

Facebook and Twitter can help you grow your network just as well as LinkedIn can, but there's a major difference. The former two networks can consist of just about anybody – from vendors you do business with every day, to people who simply "Follow" and "Like" anyone they happen to come across. You could end up with a great deal of people following you, that aren't actually *following* you. Maybe they've hid your news feed, or they simply don't read the tweets you send out because they don't care. Other than building their own follower list, they're not really interested in you.

However, every single member of LinkedIn is there for one reason and one reason only: to grow and market themselves or their business. Small businesses are using it to keep in touch with vendors and clients, all the while gaining new vendors and clients. Individuals are there to build a resume, to find work, or to create networks and build contacts that they can use later down the road. LinkedIn gives you all the social media benefits of building and growing your network, but it lets you target that network and create it out of other professionally-minded individuals and businesses.

Keeping in touch with your customers

Historically, focus groups used to be one of the main ways companies kept in touch with their customers and found out what they were saying about their products. Today focus groups are almost a thing of the past-primarily for one reason: social networking allows companies to keep in direct contact with their customers in a way like never before. While keeping in touch with your customers is one of the benefits that can be found by using Facebook and Twitter – you can also find it using LinkedIn.

Hiring new employees

Remember that many people who use LinkedIn are not small business owners, but are looking for a small business to work for – and yours could be just the one. LinkedIn allows you to perform an in-depth search on a person's employment background, education history and industry experience. LinkedIn even goes one step further and will localize the search for you, so it's just a matter of calling that person across town and setting up an interview. With LinkedIn some companies might find that they can do away with advertising in the classifieds altogether.

Check out what your competitors are doing

Many business owners have already developed a LinkedIn profile for their business and more are beginning to every day. The chances that your competitors are on LinkedIn are good and this gives you another opportunity to find out what they're doing, what campaigns they're running, what they're offering to customers and how you can continue to be better than them. Worried that they won't want to be part of your LinkedIn network? Don't worry about that – they're going to want to keep up with what you're doing too!

Keep up with industry trends

Unlike other social networking sites, this doesn't mean keeping up to date on news and happenings within the industry. Rather, LinkedIn gives you a full, in-depth look at what your industry is doing and looks at what the current trends are and where they're headed. For instance, LinkedIn allows you to see what the average age of a person in your industry is, how large your industry is compared with others and how it's growing compared with your competition.

Increase your online reviews

Lots of business owners know how important online reviews are and LinkedIn is a great way to build the number of reviews you have online for your business. One of the unique features of LinkedIn is that you can recommend other people and give them referrals and they can do the same for you. When people search for your industry or a product or service your company provides, they'll be looking for these reviews and will easily be able to find them. And, because LinkedIn pages generally get very high page rankings in search engines, people will find those reviews whether they're browsing LinkedIn – or outside of it.

Some business owners join LinkedIn thinking that it's a simple matter of setting up a profile and waiting for the profits to roll in. But while it's true that LinkedIn can help increase your revenue, buying into this or any of the other common myths about using LinkedIn is the biggest obstacle that keep businesses from being successful. In the next section, we'll look at what those myths are.

Misconceptions about LinkedIn

Unfortunately, sometimes business owners join LinkedIn only to be disappointed that they don't get the results they were expecting (especially after hearing about everything the social networking site can do for them). Most often it's not the fault of the website, but that of the business owner, either because their hopes were too high or because they don't really understand how to use the site.

Here are the biggest misconceptions that many small business owners have about using LinkedIn and how they block their path to success.

With LinkedIn, recruiters are no longer necessary

Recruiters and head-hunters have long been a necessary part of business and there's no need for a company to eliminate the role of their recruiter just because they've joined LinkedIn. It's true that LinkedIn will lay a multitude of resumes and prospects at your feet. That may be enough for your company and you *may* be able to stop outsourcing your recruiting needs. However, if you have very specific needs and are looking for "that certain someone," you may still want to keep the human touch a recruiter will bring. You need to look at your business and determine whether or not you can use just LinkedIn, or if you need to use both.

There's no need to fill out the whole profile on LinkedIn

This is one of the biggest reasons why businesses don't succeed when using LinkedIn to market themselves. It's the equivalent of putting together an entire television commercial and then forgetting to include the name of the product you're selling. The whole point of LinkedIn is to get you, your name, your brand, and anything you can possibly say about your brand out there in front of people's eyes. If you don't seize the opportunity and take the two minutes to fill out your entire profile, then just about every minute you do spend on LinkedIn will be a waste of time. In the next section we'll look at how to properly fill out your profile to make sure that you make the most out of it.

Thousands of connections = thousands of opportunities

The whole point of LinkedIn is to target your social media marketing to professionals and like-minded people. So if you own a sporting goods business and have one thousand connections to different suppliers, vendors, clients, and good leads, they very well could turn into one thousand opportunities. However, if half of those are people who want to connect simply just to connect and they have nothing to do with you or sporting goods, they will probably amount to nothing. The number of connections doesn't equal the number of opportunities; the quality of those connections does. A little later in this guide, we'll tell you how can make the most of your connections and to make sure they're of the highest quality.

LinkedIn is the best social networking site for my business

This isn't necessarily a myth. LinkedIn *might* be the best social networking for your site; Facebook, Twitter, or YouTube might also be better. It's up to you, or a social media marketing professional, to assess all the different sites, as well as your business, and determine which social media site is best for your company. No one site is going to be the best for every single company and depending on things like target audiences the best site for one company may not be the best site for the other. Even if LinkedIn isn't the *best* social networking site for your business, it's still a *good* one, and you should still be a part of it. We'll touch on this later on in the guide if and when you're looking for a social media expert to help you with your LinkedIn campaign.

You need to post updates as often, and as much, as you can

This simply isn't true and can actually annoy those in your network. Update after update is most irritating when they're constant self-promotion, redundant, or just plain pointless. Again, it's quality over quantity. We'll touch on this later on in this guide and tell you about when and how often you should be posting.

Now that we've dispelled the myths that will keep you from being successful on LinkedIn, what exactly do you need to do in order to be a success?

Getting LinkedIn

You know the benefits of using LinkedIn to market your small business and you now realize some of the misconceptions that come with the site, and the truth about them. But how exactly do you join LinkedIn and what do you do once you're there? You take advantage of it, not to only get your name out there and promote your brand, but also to create joint ventures and get new leads! While it can be time-consuming, is the only way to fully maximize LinkedIn to its potential and this section tells you how to do it.

Setting up your profile

Joining LinkedIn is easy, but a bit more involved than joining other social networks. Go to www.linkedin.com start by filling out the simple form on the LinkedIn home page. Here you'll be asked about your name, email address and the password you'd like to have for your account. After this you'll be asked to fill out a slightly longer form that will include your job title, employer's name, and your geographic location. LinkedIn will send you an email with a link included that you'll need to click on in order to confirm your email address. Lastly, you'll need to decide whether you want a free account or paid account.

Premium LinkedIn accounts, or those you pay for, will give you more detailed search results, allow you to message people you're not connected with, but when you're just getting started, it's best to use a free account. You'll be able to get the feel of the website without having to pay a price for it, and you can decide if you like it, or if you'd even use those features you'll be paying extra for.

Remember that when you sign up for LinkedIn, not only must you use your real name, as a requirement of the site, but it only makes sense to. After all, you're on the site in order to grow your networks and promote your business. You definitely want people to know who you really are!

Throughout the process of setting up your profile you'll be asked whether you want to start making connections, or to add the names of friends you'd like to invite. For now it's best to skip these steps, as they take time and you can always come back to them later. Not only will you want to take the time to complete these steps when needed, but you also want to focus on just getting your profile set up first.

Making connections

Never underestimate the power of connections on LinkedIn; they are pretty much the entire reason why you joined in the first place. After you've set up your account, you'll be taken to your profile page. At the very top you'll see several different tabs including Profile, Jobs, Interests, and Connections. Click on Connections and you'll be given several options to see who you already know on LinkedIn via email. All you have to do is enter your email address and click on "Continue". You'll be taken to a screen asking for your permission to access your profile page and your email accounts. You'll need to grant this permission if you want LinkedIn to find people you already know and make connection suggestions, but you can always go back and change it later if you're uncomfortable with LinkedIn having access to that information.

Once LinkedIn checks all of the email addresses in your contact list and compares it with their database (it takes about five seconds), you can simply start checking off all the people you already know that you'd like to connect with. You can skip this step, but you shouldn't. It's a great place to get started meeting people on LinkedIn. Once you've selected who you want to connect with, click on the button that says, "Add selected connections".

Once you've added those connections you'll then have the option to connect with people that are in your contact list, but are not yet on LinkedIn. You can check as many as you'd like off, and then again click "Add selected to network". The people you've selected will be sent an invitation by LinkedIn to join and connect with you.

After LinkedIn has checked one of your email addresses, they will give you the option of checking your other email accounts, and either adding connections or sending invitations just as you did with the first email address. LinkedIn will go through all of the accounts with you, to make sure they're getting all of your contacts.

After LinkedIn has checked through all of your email accounts looking for contacts, check the box that says, "See more connections." After doing this LinkedIn will pull up a number of profiles for you that you may or may not know. These might be past co-workers, clients, employers, or people you know personally. Underneath each profile you'll see a box saying "Connect". Simply start connecting with those you want to!

If you feel as though it will benefit you, you can also search for past alumni on LinkedIn to connect with. Just hover over the Connections tab at the top and click on the "Search Alumni" option from the drop-down menu. If you haven't done so yet, you'll need to fill in the information of your past college or university, as well as the dates you attended, the field of study, and what degree you received (or will receive).

Remember, it's quality over quantity. Just because someone may have been your best friend 30 years ago, if they're not in your industry and not interested in your industry, you may not need to make the connection. Remember that every connection could be a potential lead, but you don't want to have too many connections as this could create a confusing cluster of networks that don't really have a lot of lead potential.

Joining Groups

What are groups and why are they important? Different companies or individuals create groups that anyone can join and meet with more people. Anyone can join a group and if you meet someone in that group that you want to talk to, you can send them a private message if you're not connected to them.

To join groups, look at the tabs located at the top of the page. Hover over the "Interests" tab and then click on "Groups" from the drop-down menu. Once you do you'll be given a list of groups that are recommended for you, based on your profile and contact information. Simply click on the groups you'd like to join and you're in! If you don't see anything that interests you, you can click on "Find a group" to find a specific one, or

"Create a group" if you don't find anything relevant to what you're looking for.

Under the "Interests" tab you'll also be able to choose "Companies" which will give you a listing of companies that you're following or might be interested in. Not only can you follow these companies, but you can also create a company page for your own business, which will be a huge step towards promoting your brand.

Just like you can find new brands and promote your own business under "Companies", you can also do so by clicking on "Pulse", also located in the drop-down menu under Interests. Pulse is a section of LinkedIn that lets you check out news, tips, articles, and blog posts that might be of interest to you. Again, you can also create and publish your own blog post, whether it's a how-to article, a tips and trick article, or an article stating the benefits of your business' product or service. This will also promote your business, just by using LinkedIn.

Just like Pulse, you can also check out what people are sharing – and share your own content – using SlideShare, one of the newer features of LinkedIn. SlideShare includes interesting and helpful information, but in the form of infographics, slide shows, and other visual mediums. This is what makes LinkedIn sort of a combination of Facebook and Instagram!

If it's increasing your education you're interested in, you can do so by clicking on either "Education" or "Online Learning." Either of these will lead you through the process of getting the education you want.

Create joint ventures

If you're new to the world of joint ventures, they're a relationship that you form with another business in which you both promote each other so that you both benefit. Whether you're looking for your first joint venture, or you're just looking to add to your list of JVs, LinkedIn is a great place to find them! When looking for JVs you want to partner with businesses that are related to your industry, but that are not your direct competition. So for example, if you own the sporting goods store mentioned before you wouldn't want to joint venture with other sporting goods stores. But, you might want to think about joint ventures with a ski resort in the area, or even the professional hockey team that resides in town.

LinkedIn is especially good at creating opportunities for joint ventures because of the highly keyword-targeted search found within the website. This feature allows you to significantly narrow down your search and find potential joint ventures that are best for you. It not only allows you to search for keywords that you *do* want, but also keywords that you *don't*. Using the sporting goods store example again, you could not only search for "ski resorts," but also "ski resorts NOT ski shops," or you could write, "New York hockey teams NOT New York hockey stores." You can also consolidate the keywords and narrow your search even more by using the keyword "OR." So you could search for possible joint ventures by searching for "ski resorts OR New York hockey teams NOT stores," and you'd get a highly-targeted list of possible joint venture partnerships that could turn into huge profits and revenue.

Believe it or not, this is just the tip of the iceberg when it comes to joining and using, LinkedIn. While these are some of the biggest ways to use LinkedIn to its full potential and really rev up your revenue, there are many other numerous tips and tricks you can use to ensure further success when using LinkedIn to market your small business. The next section will look at what those are.

Quick Tips for Success

While LinkedIn doesn't have all the unnecessary games and apps that Facebook has (and that can be quite distracting,) LinkedIn is still so much more than just setting up a profile and joining groups. To make sure you get the most out of using LinkedIn to market your small business, here are some quick tips for success.

- Put your LinkedIn URL on every piece of marketing material you distribute, right in front of your Twitter and Facebook URLs. You want people to be able to contact you in any way possible and in such a digital age LinkedIn is becoming one of the most popular ways to connect.

- Join groups. This time be specific. Join groups of organizations and associations that govern your industry or are related to it. It will show that you're interested in staying on top of industry news and trends and will help grow your network.

- Once in a while, update your status with samples of recent work. If your photography studio has a blog, you could post a "Favorite Picture of the Week" every week and then use the widget to import the blog post into LinkedIn. Then, use the actual picture as your status update.

- Always upload your LinkedIn statuses to your Facebook and Twitter accounts (and any other social networking sites you belong to). It's a great way to get the word out to everyone all at once.

- Don't just join groups, start one! Start a group under the name of your company, your website, or your brand. Invite people to join and try to make it as active as possible by taking polls, asking questions to generate interest and by generally interacting with clients. When speaking on groups that belong to others always invite them to join yours.

- Be active in the groups you do join – this can't be stressed enough. It's the entire reason you joined the group in the first place. Talk to people as much as possible, answer questions, research for answers and send links (a mix of your website and others). Be as active as you can and people will remember you for it.
- Don't spend a lot of time directly selling or pushing your product. People come to you for help and because they think you have something of value to them – not because they want to look at advertisements all the time. Spend time helping those people and they'll soon become your customers.
- Stuck on what to post as your status? Press releases, recommendations, links to helpful blog posts, quick tips, quotes, and links to YouTube videos are just a few ideas to help get you started.
- Update your status once a week.
- Remember to keep your LinkedIn profile up to date. What you enter the day you join may not be the information you'd enter two years after joining. Every couple of months go back into your profile settings and see if there's anything you'd like to add or change.
- Customize your public profile URL. Just like you can change the URL of your page on Facebook, you can also change it on LinkedIn. If you don't do this, new connections, groups, and other companies can't easily find you because your URL looks like this: www.linkedin.com/mycompanyabc23459738492. You can customize this though and make it look more professional, as well easier to find, by simply changing it to: www.linkedin.com/companyabc.
- After some of their most recent changes, LinkedIn started to include cover photos in their profiles. Taking the time to do so is important and should be done so that connections can get to know your personality, and to promote your business.
- Create a Profile Badge for your personal website or blog. This is a badge provided by LinkedIn that you can post on your website so that people can easily connect with you on LinkedIn.

LinkedIn Checklist

If you have a specific vision for your LinkedIn profile and marketing campaign, or you're already handling an involved campaign, joining the site is easy and maintaining your presence is fairly simple. But there is a lot involved and you want to make sure you don't miss a single step. Here's a checklist to make sure that you get the most important steps in.

- ❑ Join by going to www.linkedin.com and entering your name and email information.

- ❑ Create an interesting and detailed profile that includes as much information as possible about you and your company. Use all the tips from this guide to help you create your profile.

- ❑ Choose a photo to display that best represents your company and make sure you don't go any further until you do. You're invisible otherwise.

- ❑ Make connections with people in your email address book. Then continue to make connections through suggestions, Companies, and Groups.

- ❑ Ask for recommendations from past customers who had a good experience with you and who you feel comfortable asking to share their experience. Get three recommendations as soon as possible.

- ❑ Give recommendations! When you use a product or a business give them a recommendation. If someone asks for one and you feel they deserve one, give it to them.

- ❑ Integrate your LinkedIn profile with your blog and with all your other social media marketing campaigns.

❑ Put your LinkedIn URL on business cards, stationery and any other marketing materials you're going to use for your business.

❑ If you don't think you have the time to set up and maintain your LinkedIn profile, much less integrate it with your social media marketing campaign, you can hire a marketing consultant to do it for you. There are many things you need to look for when hiring a consultant. In the next section we'll look at the most important questions you should ask anyone you're considering hiring.

Questions You Should Ask

You'll probably have lots of questions to ask your social media consultant. Here's a list to get you started on the ones that are most important.

1. What is your expertise with LinkedIn?
Because your consultant will most likely be doing more for you than just working on your LinkedIn account, you can ask how long they've been using LinkedIn professionally or how many clients they have set up profiles for. Listen for answers that include the direction they took client's profile in and how they used it to boost their profits.

2. Can you give me an example of a small business like mine you helped with LinkedIn?
Often LinkedIn profiles can be viewed without actually connecting with them. Your consultant should be able to give you the name of at least one company that you can check out on LinkedIn. Look for yourself how successful they are on it.

3. What's the biggest mistake you've seen a small business make with LinkedIn?
The worst answer you could get here is "nothing." Mostly, you're asking this question to see whether or not they could identify problems when they came up and if they could solve them.

4. How will you know if my LinkedIn marketing campaign is working?
They might have any number of answers here referring to tracking software and analytics and that's all good. What you don't want is someone who says, "I guarantee to get you 1,000 new connections" because essentially that means nothing.

5. How are you going to help us?

You might think that this is a question for the consultant to ask you, but it's actually not. Marketing consultants, social media consultants, Internet marketing consultants – they go by a thousand names and they will each focus on particular aspects of social media marketing. You need to know which areas they're going to focus on, or whether they'll do it all for you.

6. Do you know HTML code?

It used to be that only web designers needed to know HTML code but today, social media marketing has become so diverse and includes so many things that anyone who's doing any type of social media marketing for you needs to know at least the basics.

7. Can I have at least three references and can I contact them?

If they can't provide you with references you shouldn't hire them.

Conclusion

While it may take a little time and effort to create a marketing strategy using LinkedIn, the process could be very rewarding for your company. If you are able to connect with more customers and generate more leads your business could see an increase in profits. When you need help getting onto LinkedIn call your local marketing consultant and ask how they can help. Then go through the questions mentioned in this guide and find the one that can bring your social media presence to life!

Next Steps

Thank you for reading this book. We hope that you found it useful and it has given you the information you need to use LinkedIn to market your business.

If you would like additional assistance, please contact us at:

www.LinkedInsiderMarketing.com

Recommended Resources

Business Owners, Entrepreneurs, & Authors as Media Experts?

You know how its hard to get into national publications like NBC, CBS, ABC, & Fox so you can become a celebrity in your field of expertise?

I solve this.

I do this by utilizing a special insiderwebsite and a unique press release format to guarantee this for any serious professional, you will have a LinkedIn profile picture just like mine which will get them to chose you every time.

To become a cited media expert, go now to:

www.LinkedInsiderMarketing.com

Linked University - The Definitive Training Program for Building Your Business on LinkedIn

What our University training will do for your business:

1) Establish yourself as the authority or expert in your space.

2) Put a system in place to generate consistent leads for your business.

3) Increase sales.

Our, at-your-pace training includes step-by-step video tutorials, workbooks, templates, and audio training for when you're on the go. Membership includes new releases to keep you in the loop on critical LinkedIn updates, as well as new sales strategies and tactics that we release only to our members.

Monthly live group coaching offers all of our members the opportunity to get personal assistance with their LinkedIn marketing efforts and overall online marketing strategies.

We also feature monthly expert interviews featuring leading sales and marketing experts, providing even further training for you to develop the most powerful marketing system possible.

For free LinkedIn training videos and to explore if membership is right for you visit:

www.LinkedUniversity.net

How to Get LinkedIn Leads Everyday with
Less Than 20-Minutes of Effort

www.LinkedInsider.net

How to set up a simple system within LinkedIn that consistently generates leads and opportunities!

An easy to use and mostly automated LinkedIn drip marketing system to keep you top-of-mind with thousands of prospects.

How to attract new clients from this network within months!! With this training you'll have a repeatable system for landing new clients.

Bonus Training: All attendees will receive over an hour of step-by-step training on optimizing your LinkedIn profile.

You'll also get access to our LinkedIn ROI calculator, so you'll know exactly what kind of return you can expect from these efforts.

To get LinkedIn leads everyday with minimal effort, go to:

www.LinkedInsider.net

www.ingramcontent.com/pod-product-compliance
Lightning Source LLC
Chambersburg PA
CBHW071832200526
45169CB00018B/1415